WITHDRAWN

Manteno Public Library District
50 West Division Street
Manteno, Illinois 60950

A Kid's Guide to Drawing™

How to Draw Cartoon Symbols of the United States of America

Curt Visca and Kelley Visca

The Rosen Publishing Group's
PowerKids Press™
New York

Dedicated to the Lord, who's blessed us with talent and children. God bless the USA!

Published in 2004 by The Rosen Publishing Group, Inc.
29 East 21st Street, New York, NY 10010

First Edition

Editor: Natashya Wilson
Book Design: Kim Sonsky
Layout Design: Michael J. Caroleo

Illustration Credits: All illustrations © Curt Visca.
Photo Credits: Cover and pp. 6, 8, 12, 20 © Eye Wire; p. 10 © Bill Ross/CORBIS; pp. 14, 16 © Bettmann/CORBIS; p.18 photo by Thaddeus Harden.

Visca, Curt.
How to draw cartoon symbols of the United States of America / Curt Visca and Kelley Visca.— 1st ed.
    p. cm. — (A kid's guide to drawing)
Summary: Provides facts about eight symbols of the United States, as well as step-by-step instructions for drawing cartoons of each one.
Includes bibliographical references and index.
ISBN 0-8239-6727-1
1. United States—In art—Juvenile literature. 2. Drawing—Technique—Juvenile literature. [1. United States in art. 2. Drawing—Technique 3. Cartooning—Technique.] I. Visca, Kelley. II. Title. III. Series.
NC655 .V58 2004

2002010400

Manufactured in the United States of America

CONTENTS

Cartoon Symbols of the United States of America

The United States of America was **founded** on the ideas of liberty, justice, and equality. This means that the people who live in the United States live freely and are treated fairly. The government is a **democracy**. American citizens vote to decide who the leaders should be and which rules should be made into laws.

Many American citizens are **patriotic**. They love their country and are proud to live there. Many people who live in other countries **emigrate**, or move, to the United States to gain freedom and equality.

This book will teach you about eight different **symbols** that represent America and that make people think of the United States of America. You will learn about the history behind the symbols and how to draw a cartoon of each one.

A cartoon is a simple picture of an object or a person, drawn to make people laugh. Cartoon drawings include only the most important lines and shapes. They are easy and fun to draw.

As you follow the steps for drawing each cartoon symbol, be sure to turn to the Terms for Drawing Cartoons on page 22 for names and pictures of the drawing shapes and terms. New parts of each drawing are shown in red.

You will need the following supplies to draw cartoon symbols of the United States of America:

- Paper
- A sharp pencil or a felt-tipped marker
- An eraser
- Colored pencils or crayons to add color

When you draw your cartoons, sit at a desk or a table in a quiet place. Make sure that there is plenty of light and that you have all your supplies handy.

Remember to take your time, try your best, and practice your cartoons over and over again. It won't take long for you to become a patriotic cartoonist!

The American Flag

The American flag is the official flag of the United States. The **Continental Congress** adopted the first American flag on June 14, 1777. June 14 is celebrated as Flag Day every year.

The Continental Congress chose the colors red, white, and blue for the American flag. Red stands for strength and bravery, white for goodness, and blue for justice. The flag has 13 **horizontal** stripes. Seven are red and six are white. They **represent** the original 13 colonies and rays of sunlight. The upper left-hand corner of the flag, called the **canton**, is a blue rectangle with 50 five-pointed stars. The stars represent the 50 states, and also the heavens. The American flag has had 50 stars since Hawaii became the fiftieth state in 1960. The flag is also known as the Stars and Stripes, Old Glory, and the Star-Spangled Banner, the title of America's national **anthem**.

1

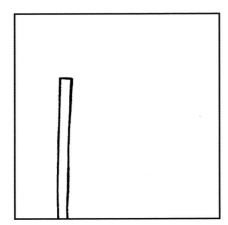

Please begin by drawing two long vertical lines and one short horizontal line for the flagpole.

2

Draw four curved lines for the bottom of the eagle. Draw a curved line and four letter *U*'s for each wing. Make a curved line, a straight line, and a sideways letter *V* for the head.

3

Give your cartoon flag a face. Draw two circles and two dots for eyes. Make a curved rectangle around the eyes. Add a nose. Make a thick letter *U* and two lines for the mouth.

4

Next draw the outline of the flag by making slightly curved lines on the top, right side, and bottom. Make seven thick lines inside the flag to show the stripes.

5

Add as many stars as you can in the canton. Can you fit all 50?

6

Add action lines, detail on the eagle, and curved lines for a cloud. I stand and salute you!

7

The Bald Eagle

The bald eagle was chosen as a symbol of the United States in 1782. It represents freedom and power, and lives only in North

America. Not everyone wanted the bald eagle to be the national bird. Benjamin Franklin thought that the turkey was a better choice. He wrote that the turkey is "a much more respectable bird."

The bald eagle's head and tail feathers are white. Bald eagles can grow to be 3 feet (1 m) long from head to tail with a wingspan of 8 feet (2.5 m). They live in nests called **aeries**, which they build in trees and on cliffs. They eat mostly fish. In the 1970s, there were only from 2,000 to 3,000 bald eagles left. Hunters and **pesticides** had killed many of them. People made laws to protect these beautiful birds. There are now more than 100,000 bald eagles.

1

Draw an oval, a curved line, and two shaded circles for the eyes. Make a wavy, sideways letter V, a short straight line, and a letter C for the beak.

2

Outstanding! Make a thin rectangle with a curvy rectangle on top for the hat. Add straight lines and stars. Draw curved lines and small letter U's to finish the head.

3

Next make three slightly curved lines for the sleeve. Make three letter U's for the wing. Draw a curved line and a short horizontal line for the bald eagle's chest.

4

Next add a sideways letter V for the other sleeve. Draw letter U's for the wing. Make curved lines and straight lines for the front leg and a sideways letter V for the back leg.

5

Draw wiggly lines for the leg feathers. Make a curvy, sideways letter V and curved lines for the feet. Make sharp talons on the ends of the toes. Add three tail feathers.

6

Add stars and detail to finish your cartoon. You have an eagle eye!

The Statue of Liberty

The Statue of Liberty stands 151 feet 1 inch (46 m) high on Liberty Island in Upper New York Bay. It was a gift of friendship from France, given to the United States in 1884. It is made of 31 tons (28 t) of hammered copper sheets. The statue is of a woman. The torch held in her right hand represents liberty. Her

left hand holds a tablet with "July 4, 1776" written on it, the date on which the United States declared its **independence** from England. The crown on her head has seven spikes. It stands for the world's seven seas and continents. The statue's robe would equal 4,000 square yards (3,345 sq m) of fabric if it were real. At her feet is a broken chain that stands for **tyranny**. About two million people visit the statue each year. It is a symbol of freedom to people around the world.

1

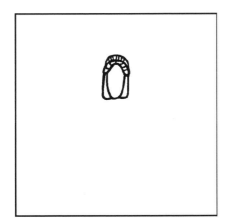

Start with a letter *U*. Make two bent lines and a curved oval shape for hair. Add curved lines inside it. Make a curved line on top for the crown. Draw straight lines inside it.

2

Make dots for eyes and lines for eyelashes. Draw a nose. Make a line with two curved lines above it and a *U* below it for the mouth. Add seven upside-down *V*'s for the spikes.

3

Make a curvy sleeve, then straight lines for the arm. Add a *C* and three ovals for the hand. Draw a *U* and circles for the torch handle. Add rectangles and spiky lines for the torch.

4

Make a letter *U* for the neck. Draw bent lines and wavy lines to make the robe. Make the tablet using straight lines. Make the hand using a wiggly line and a curved line.

5

Amazing! Add small letter *U*'s for toes and a curved line for each sandal. Use curved and straight lines to draw the stand.

6

Add detail on the statue. Make trees, a boat, water, buildings, a flag, and a cloud.

The Liberty Bell

The Liberty Bell is displayed in Philadelphia, Pennsylvania. It weighs about 2,080 pounds (943.5 kg) and is made mostly

of copper. It arrived in Philadelphia from England in 1752. It cracked when it was rung! In 1753, John Pass and John Stow of Philadelphia remade it. Their last names are on the front of the bell. "Philada," for Philadelphia, and MDCCLIII, the year 1753, appear below the names. For many years the bell rang to call people together for special events. It rang on July 8, 1776, for the first public reading of the **Declaration of Independence**. People who fought against slavery were the first to call it the Liberty Bell, around 1839. In 1846, a 28-inch (71-cm) crack appeared in the bell. It hasn't been rung since. Every July 4, the Liberty Bell is tapped gently to honor Independence Day.

1

Let's begin by making two circles and two dots for the eyes. Add a letter *C* for the nose. Make a thick letter *U* with two short straight lines at the ends for the mouth.

2

Next make two wavy lines for the sides of the Liberty Bell. Add a curved line at the bottom to connect both sides. Make a small letter *U* on the bottom right.

3

You are fantastic! Draw three curved lines on the bottom of the bell for detail. Make a thick bent line to show the crack in the Liberty Bell. Add a dot to show a bolt in the crack.

4

Draw a long line over the bell. Add curved lines on top. Make a vertical line, a horizontal line, and a bent line on each side. Make two circles and a short line. Add lines for the ties.

5

You are the best! Make two straight lines for each arm. Add shading on each arm for detail. Draw five curved lines on each hand for fingers.

6

Add action lines and detail. Write "PASS AND STOW," "Philada," and "MDCCLIII." A+!

George Washington

George Washington is known as the Father of Our Country. He was born on February 22, 1732, and was the first president of the United States. He grew up in Virginia and married Martha Dandridge Custis in 1759. Washington fought in both the **French and Indian War** and the **American Revolution**. In June 1775, he became commander in chief of the Continental army. He led the army for six years during the Revolution, until America was free from British rule. In 1787, Washington helped other U.S. leaders to write the Constitution, the rules for running the United States. That year, Washington was **unanimously** elected president of the United States. He served for eight years. He died on December 14, 1799. Today people can visit his home, called Mount Vernon, in Virginia.

1

You'll like this drawing, by George! Begin by making a letter C for George Washington's head. Add wiggly lines around the head for his hair.

2

Make an oval and a dot for each eye. Draw a curved line for the nose. Make a straight line and a letter U for the mouth. Put a line on the side. Add shading to show the tongue.

3

Nice! Make a curved wiggly line for a ruffled collar. Draw a curved line, a bent line, and a straight line for each side of the collar. Make straight lines for rest of the jacket.

4

Next make make a long, curvy line for the pants. Draw a letter L, an upside-down letter V, and a backward letter L for the coattails.

5

Well done! Draw a wiggly line for each ruffled shirt cuff. Make a curved line for each thumb, finger, and palm. Draw straight and curved lines for the ankles and shoes.

6

Complete your drawing by adding detail and action lines. Beautiful work!

Uncle Sam

Uncle Sam is a cartoon character that was first used to symbolize the U.S. government during the **War of 1812**. Many historians believe that Uncle Sam was named for Samuel Wilson, a meat packer during the War of 1812. He shipped meat to the

U.S. Army in barrels stamped with the initials "U.S." When the meat arrived, the soldiers said it came from "Uncle Sam," which became a nickname for the U.S. government. Political cartoonist Thomas Nast drew some of the earliest cartoons of Uncle Sam in the 1800s. The most famous picture of Uncle Sam appears on the poster shown above, from **World War I**. The poster was painted by James Montgomery Flagg in 1916–1917.

1

Draw a curved shape and three curved lines for the hat. Add a line and a star. Under the hat, draw two curved lines on each side. Add ears and two more curved lines for cheeks.

2

Make circles and dots for the eyes. Add a letter U for the nose. Draw a thick curved line and two straight lines for the mouth. Add wiggly lines for the beard and hair.

3

Draw a circle and two curved lines for the tie. Make a bent line, a curved line, and another bent line for each side of the collar. Add three vertical lines and two short lines under the tie.

4

You are creative! Next draw three straight lines for each jacket sleeve. Make a long letter V on each side to complete Uncle Sam's jacket.

5

Draw a rectangle for each cuff. Make curved lines for the thumbs. Add a curved line and three ovals for the fingers. Draw two vertical lines and a bent line for the pants.

6

Finish your patriotic drawing by adding detail, shading, captions, and action lines.

17

The Pilgrims

The Pilgrims were a group of settlers from England. They founded Plymouth Colony in 1620, in what is now Massachusetts. This was the first lasting settlement in New England. The Pilgrims wanted to be free to practice their religion. They sailed to America on a ship called the *Mayflower*. The trip took more than two months. The Pilgrims landed at Plymouth Rock. They wrote the Mayflower Compact soon after they arrived. This paper stated that the colony would be governed, or run, by the agreement of the majority of the colonists. The Pilgrims had a hard first winter. Many of them died. The next spring, Native Americans taught the Pilgrims to grow corn and catch fish. In the fall of 1621, the Pilgrims had a good harvest. They ate a feast with the Native Americans. Today Americans celebrate Thanksgiving on the last Thursday in November to remember that meal.

1

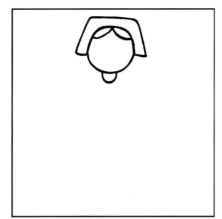

Begin by making a circle for the head, two curved lines for hair, and a letter *U* for the neck. Add bent lines for the hat.

2

Wonderful work! Draw two circles with dots inside for eyes. Add eyelashes and a letter *C* for the nose. Make a wide letter *U* with a short line at each end for the mouth.

3

Make curvy squares for the collar. Draw curved lines for the top of the shirt. Add rectangles and upside-down letter *V*'s. Make a curved line at the bottom. Add vertical lines.

4

Draw curved lines to make the fingers. Make a basket using curved lines and straight lines. Add a slightly curved line and a wiggly line for a piece of corn.

5

Nice job! Draw slightly curved lines to make the skirt and apron. Add two curved lines under the skirt for the shoes.

6

Complete your Pilgrim woman by adding detail. Draw houses, smoke, trees, and mountains!

19

Mount Rushmore

Mount Rushmore is a huge, granite sculpture of four American presidents. It is located in the Black Hills of South Dakota. The sculpture begins with  George Washington on the far left. He was America's first president. Next to him is Thomas Jefferson, who wrote the Declaration of Independence and was America's third president. Theodore Roosevelt is third. He fought against big-business **monopolies** in the early 1900s. The president on the far right is Abraham Lincoln. He helped to free slaves during the Civil War.

Mount Rushmore was designed by American sculptor Gutzon Borglum. It took more than 14 years and 400 workers to sculpt the 60-foot-tall (18-m-tall) presidents. They are each as high as a five-story building! The workers used drills and dynamite to carve the presidents. Mount Rushmore was completed in 1941. It is a popular tourist attraction.

1

Begin by drawing a bent letter C for George Washington's head. Add a curving, wiggly line around the C for his hair.

2

Next make a small letter C for Thomas Jefferson's ear. Draw a letter U for his jaw. Add wiggly lines for the top of his head and his hair.

3

Make a circle, a letter C, and two dots for Washington's eyes. Draw a letter C for his nose. Make a thick line for his mouth. Use similar shapes for Jefferson's face.

4

Draw shaggy hair for Theodore Roosevelt. Make circles, dots, and lines for his eyes and glasses. Draw lines for his head and ears. Add his nose, mustache, and mouth.

5

Draw a circle, a letter C, and dots for Lincoln's eyes. Make his nose and mouth. Add lines for his forehead and cheek. Draw wiggly lines for his hair, beard, and ear.

6

Draw eyebrows and detail. Add lines to show the mountain. Draw trees and a cloud. Perfect!

Terms for Drawing Cartoons

Here are some of the words and shapes that you need to know to draw cartoon U.S. symbols:

⟋⟋	Action lines		L	Letter *L*
∥	Angled lines		U	Letter *U*
⌐⌐	Bent lines		V	Letter *V*
◯	Circle		○	Oval
⌒	Curved line		▭	Rectangle
⌣?ᴗ"	Detail		★	Star
∴∴	Dots		☰	Straight lines
—	Horizontal line		▬	Thick line
C	Letter *C*		|	Vertical line
			〜〜	Wiggly lines

Glossary

aeries (ER-eez) Nests of birds on a cliff or a mountaintop.

American Revolution (uh-MER-uh-ken reh-vuh-LOO-shun) Battles that soldiers from the colonies fought against Britain for freedom, from 1775 to 1783.

anthem (AN-thum) A blessed or an official song or hymn.

canton (KAN-ton) The top inner corner of a flag.

Continental Congress (kon-tin-EN-tul KON-gres) A group, made up of a few people from every colony, that made decisions for the colonies.

Declaration of Independence (deh-kluh-RAY-shun UV in-duh-PEN-dints) A paper signed on July 4, 1776, declaring that the American colonies were free from British rule.

democracy (dih-MAH-kruh-see) A government that is run by the people who live under it.

emigrate (EH-mih-grayt) To leave one's country to settle in another.

founded (FOWN-did) Started.

French and Indian War (FRENCH AND IN-dee-in WOR) The battles fought between 1754 and 1763 by England, France, and Native Americans for control of North America.

horizontal (hor-ih-ZON-til) Going from side to side.

independence (in-dih-PEN-dents) Freedom from the control or support of other people.

monopolies (muh-NAH-puh-leez) Businesses owned by one group.

patriotic (pay-tree-AH-tik) Showing love for one's country.

pesticides (PES-tih-sydz) Poisons used to kill pests.

represent (reh-prih-ZENT) To stand for.

symbols (SIM-bulz) Objects or designs that stand for something else.

tyranny (TEER-uh-nee) Mean use of power over others.

unanimously (yoo-NA-nih-mus-lee) Agreeing completely.

War of 1812 (WOR UV AY-teen TWELV) A war between the United States and Britain, fought from 1812 to 1815.

World War I (WORLD WOR WUN) A war fought between the Allied Powers and the Central Powers, 1914–1918.

Index

Web Sites

Due to the changing nature of Internet links, PowerKids Press has developed an online list of Web sites related to the subject of this book. This site is updated regularly. Please use this link to access the list:
www.powerkidslinks.com/kgd/usa